JESUS

A very brief history

HELEN K. BOND

First published in Great Britain in 2017

Society for Promoting Christian Knowledge
36 Causton Street
London SW1P 4ST
www.spck.org.uk

Copyright © Helen K. Bond 2017

All rights reserved. No part of this book may be reproduced or transmitted in any form
or by any means, electronic or mechanical, including photocopying, recording, or by any
information storage and retrieval system, without permission in writing from the publisher.

SPCK does not necessarily endorse the individual views contained in its publications.

Gospel of Thomas quotations are taken from the translation by Stephen Patterson and
Marvin Meyer at <http://gnosis.org/naghamm/gosthom.html>.

Unless otherwise stated, Scripture quotations are from the ESV® Bible (The Holy Bible,
English Standard Version®), copyright © 2001 by Crossway, a publishing ministry of Good
News Publishers. All rights reserved.

British Library Cataloguing-in-Publication Data
A catalogue record for this book is available from the British Library

ISBN 978–0–281–07599–7
eBook ISBN 978–0–281–07600–0

Typeset by Manila Typesetting Company
First printed in Great Britain by Ashford Colour Press
Subsequently digitally printed in Great Britain

eBook by Manila Typesetting Company

Produced on paper from sustainable forests

To my family –
Keith, Katriona and Scotty –
with all my love

Contents

Chronology

Chronology

Introduction

Around the year 30 CE, in an insignificant eastern province of the Roman Empire, a Jewish prophet met with a brutal and shameful end on a Roman cross. Up in Galilee, Jesus of Nazareth had caused a stir with his revolutionary preaching and his exceptional abilities as a healer and exorcist. He'd gathered crowds of followers and brought his message to the city of Jerusalem, just as it was packed to bursting with pilgrims at the busy Passover season. And the Roman governor, fearing a riot, had ordered his arrest and execution.

In the normal course of things, that would have been the end of the affair. Jesus was not the first would-be Jewish messiah, nor would he be the last. What distinguished him from all the others, however, were the claims of his disciples that God had raised him from the dead, that he was now seated with the Almighty in heaven, and that his death and resurrection had opened up a new way for all people to relate to the God of Israel. These were claims that would only intensify over time, eventually leading his followers to break away from their Jewish roots and, with the addition now of non-Jewish converts, to form what would eventually become the world's largest religion, Christianity.

This short book provides a sketch of what we know about Jesus and his legacy. The first half will look at the historical man, the Galilean Jew who lived in a homeland dominated by Rome. We'll look at Jesus' Jewish heritage, his miracles and message, friends and enemies, and eventual execution.

In the second half of the book we'll look at Jesus' legacy, starting with the differing accounts of his life in the New Testament texts. We'll look too at portrayals of Jesus that weren't included in the Bible, both those deemed perfectly orthodox and those that weren't. We'll see how the conversion of Constantine advanced the Christian message, and consider the transformation of a Jewish prophet into a Gentile God and the subsequent spread of Jesus devotion throughout the Middle Ages, expressed through relics, art and the mystery plays. We'll look at Jesus in the religions of the world – not just the Christian faith but also his exalted place in Islam and ambiguous role within Judaism. Finally we'll look at Jesus in the modern secular West, at his depiction in film and novels, and at the phenomenon of 'cultural Christianity'.

First, though, we need to ask the most basic questions of all. Did Jesus really exist? And if so, where should we find the most reliable sources to reconstruct his life?

Part 1

JESUS OF NAZARETH

1

Did Jesus exist?

In 1909 a German thinker, Arthur Drews (pronounced 'Drefs'), caused a stir with his highly controversial claim that Jesus had never lived. In *The Christ Myth*, Drews argued that what mattered to Christians was not the 'Jesus of history' but the individual's personal encounter in the present with the risen Jesus. The historical Jesus, he claimed, was nothing but a myth, developed first by Paul and later expanded by the Evangelists. Although Drews' views never commanded much scholarly support, they proved remarkably persistent. Similar ideas were put forward in the 1970s by G. A. Wells (though he modified his views later), and 'mythicist' theories still abound today on the internet. Indeed, in a recent poll, 25 per cent of 18–34-year-olds in the UK thought that Jesus was a mythical or fictional character.

In fact ancient evidence for Jesus is remarkably early and widespread. It is true that no member of the Roman elite mentions him before the early second century, but this is not particularly surprising. Romans were generally distrustful of 'new' religions; they took note of Jesus and the movement that followed him only when it threatened to disrupt society, and would hardly have lowered themselves to probe too carefully into its origins. Our earliest Roman reference to Jesus comes from the historian Tacitus. In a famous passage in which he describes Nero's brutal persecution of Christians following the fire of Rome in the mid 60s CE, Tacitus gives an all too brief account of Christian origins. Victims, he explains, took their name from *Christus* [i.e. Christ], 'who had undergone the death penalty in the reign of Tiberius, by sentence of the procurator Pontius Pilate'.[1]

Jewish evidence for Jesus is earlier, though not entirely straightforward. The Jewish historian Josephus mentions Jesus in his account of Jewish history, written at the very end of the first century:

> About this time there lived Jesus, a wise man, *if indeed one ought to call him a man*. For he was one who wrought surprising feats and was a teacher of such people as accept the truth gladly. He won over many Jews and many of the Greeks. *He was the Messiah*. When Pilate, upon hearing him accused by men of the highest standing amongst us, had condemned him to be crucified, those who had in the first place come to love him did not give up their affection for him. *On the third day he appeared to them restored to life, for the prophets of God had prophesied these and countless other marvellous things about him*. And the tribe of the Christians, so called after him, has still to this day not disappeared.[2]

Josephus was a Pharisaic Jew, and there is no evidence elsewhere in his writings that he had any sympathy whatsoever for the Christian movement. It seems incredible, then, that he could have written any of the phrases in italics in the above quotation. To add to the difficulty, the third-century church father Origen, who knew Josephus' works well, categorically notes that he was not a Christian – a view he could not easily have taken had he known this passage. While an earlier generation of scholars assumed that the entire paragraph was a later Christian addition, it is more common nowadays to think that it has been altered by a Christian scribe, who perhaps added the italicized sentences. Once these are removed, there is nothing that might not have been written by a first-century Jew. The original might have been something like this:

> About this time there lived Jesus, a wise man. For he was one who wrought surprising feats and was a teacher of such people as accept the truth gladly. He won over many Jews and many of the Greeks. When Pilate, upon hearing him accused by men of the highest standing amongst us, had condemned him to be crucified, those who had in the first place come to love him did not give up their affection for him. And the tribe of the Christians, so called after him, has still to this day not disappeared.

Of course, a Christian editor may also have omitted certain unfavourable parts of the paragraph. The fact that it is found within a series of 'tumults' that took place during Pilate's term of office actually suggests that the original version included something else, perhaps an account of Jesus' disturbance in the Temple (see pp. 32–4). Josephus makes certain mistakes – for instance, there is no evidence Jesus preached to Greeks – and the reference to early Christians as a 'tribe' is a peculiar one. Nevertheless, this is an extremely valuable early reference to Jesus, particularly as it comes from a Jerusalem Jew who was born only a few years after Jesus' death, who would have had access to broadly reliable information through older family members, and who might perhaps represent Jewish views of Christians at the time he wrote in late first-century Rome.

The rest of our evidence comes from Christian sources. Our earliest links with Jesus are the letters of St Paul. The great apostle founded churches throughout the eastern

Mediterranean and kept in touch with his congregations by letter, many of which are still preserved in the New Testament. All date to the 50s CE; that is, around 20 years after the death of Jesus. Although a native of Tarsus (in modern Turkey), Paul had spent time in Jerusalem and was in the city in the 30s. He knew many of Jesus' closest followers, such as Peter and other disciples, and Jesus' brother James, who took over as leader of the Jerusalem church after a vision of the risen Jesus. Clearly Paul was in an excellent position to hear reliable information about Jesus of Nazareth, and the date of his letters makes them first-rate testimony. We might wish that the great apostle had said more about the historical man. For him, the crucial aspect of Jesus' life was his death and resurrection; it is this that changes everything for Paul, and most of his letters are attempts to work out the meaning of this event, particularly for non-Jewish converts. Still, he records a number of other things about Jesus' ministry: he notes his teaching on divorce (1 Corinthians 7.10–11) and on financial support for missionaries (1 Corinthians 9.14), and his views on the end of the world (1 Thessalonians 4.15–17); and Paul provides our oldest account of the Last Supper (1 Corinthians 11.23–25).

Paul's testimony is broadly corroborated by the four New Testament Gospels, which date from around 70–100 CE. As we shall see in Part 2, the Gospels reflect the post-Easter Christian faith of the Evangelists, but this need not stop us using them as historical sources. All writing reflects the viewpoint of the author, and there never was a time when we could have had access to unbiased accounts. Even during the lifetime of Jesus, some believed in Jesus, holding him to be a prophet, a messiah and perhaps something more, while others regarded him as a charlatan or a false prophet. '

Ideally the historian would have access to all of these views and would strive to build up a picture that might account for them all. The fact that only biographies written by followers survive might make the task of sifting through the information and assessing its historical plausibility more difficult, but it is not impossible.

Of greatest importance to the historian is the Gospel of Mark. Scholars consider this to be the earliest Gospel – it was probably written just after 70 CE – and it seems to have been used as a major source by Matthew and Luke, both of whom adapted and edited it to reflect their own interests. At times we'll also need to take note of another, hypothetical document known as 'Q', from the German *Quelle*, 'source'. Although scholars are far from agreement on this matter, the dominant view is that Q represents a second source used by both Matthew and Luke. This hypothetical document can be reconstructed by isolating material shared by Matthew and Luke but not found in Mark; and it's thought to be a *written* document because the sayings found in this way are broadly in the same order. The resulting material amounts to around 70 short paragraphs, mainly consisting of sayings of Jesus. The date of Q is uncertain: scholars have put it anywhere from the 50s to the 70s, but all we know for sure is that it predates Matthew and Luke. At all events, it is a second very early witness to Jesus, and gives a good indication of the kind of things Jesus taught.

Most historical Jesus scholars are a little wary of John's Gospel. Although all the Gospels have a clear theological agenda, it seems especially pronounced in the case of John. Jesus is presented here as God incarnate, engaging in long discourses and openly discussing his status and mission with his opponents. There may of course be snippets of good historical tradition here and there, though knowing how to pinpoint them is problematic. Some scholars have given attention to texts from outside the New Testament, especially the *Gospel of Thomas* and the *Gospel of Peter*. In their present form, however, both are second-century texts and there is no solid evidence that they contain any significantly earlier material. We shall look at these gospels in more detail in Part 2.

Given that Jesus was a peasant from an insignificant part of the Empire, we actually have surprisingly good evidence not only for his existence but for the course of his life and even the contents of his teaching. All of our sources need to be used with care, but there can be no doubt that he existed and that we can say something about him. In very general terms, our best evidence for Jesus comes from Mark and Q, and these two documents will provide the basis for the following outline. Before we begin to sketch our historical portrait, however, we need to have some idea of the times in which Jesus lived.

2

Political context and early life

Our story needs to begin more than two hundred years before Jesus, with the victorious campaigns of Alexander the Great in the third century BCE. Israel was incorporated into the largest empire the world had yet known, founded not only on military conquest but on the dream of a shared language (Alexander's own native Greek) and a shared culture (a blend of Greek ideas combined with Eastern philosophy, art and beliefs known as Hellenism). Jews, like other subject peoples, seem to have been relatively happy to adopt the new ways, as long as native practices and beliefs were not compromised; and Greek forms of architecture, philosophy, government and even language seem to have slowly made their way into Israel throughout this period. Jerusalem in particular was thoroughly Hellenized; paradoxically it was also the most Jewish city in the land.

When Alexander died leaving no heirs, his empire was divided between his generals. Israel came first under the rule of the Ptolemies, based in Egypt, and then of the Seleucids, based in Syria. Around 167 BCE, however, there was a dramatic change. The Seleucid ruler Antiochus IV Epiphanes, for reasons that are not entirely clear, decided to speed up the process of Hellenization in the land. He set up a statue of Zeus in the Jerusalem Temple and outlawed the practice of the Jewish faith. Circumcision was banned, as too was abstaining from pork. Not surprisingly, violent protest soon broke out. In the Judaean town of Modein, a priestly family later known as the Maccabees (meaning 'hammer') took a stand against the king's men; they refused to sacrifice to pagan gods and fled to the hills. Taking advantage of Seleucid difficulties at home, the Maccabees gathered supporters, and first through guerrilla tactics and later on by means of a well-trained army, succeeded in establishing religious freedom and then national independence. The Maccabees set themselves up as national leaders, claiming the title of High Priest and later King. Known under their family name as the Hasmonaeans, they would rule for a century.

Despite their impressive political success, however, not everyone supported the Hasmonaeans. Although the family were priests, they did not belong to the Zadokite line, which had traditionally supplied the Jewish High Priests. The priestly group responsible for the Dead Sea Scrolls withdrew from Jerusalem into the wilderness at this period in protest at the Hasmonaean usurpation of the high priesthood. Others objected to their combination of the highest priesthood with kingship, arguing that the two roles were incompatible. But political independence guaranteed religious freedom, and most people were only too happy to exchange the hated Seleucids for native rulers.

By the mid first century BCE, however, dynastic squabbling eventually led to the end of the Hasmonaeans, and a new superpower was only too eager to assert itself in the region. In 63 BCE, the Roman general Pompey marched into Jerusalem and demanded tribute, and by 40 BCE, the Romans had installed their own man, Herod I (or Herod the Great), as King of the Jews. In many respects, Herod's was a successful reign: he presented himself as a major player on the world stage, offering gifts and benefactions through-out the eastern Mediterranean; at home he embarked on a series of impressive building projects, including a new har-bour at Caesarea on Sea and a grand refurbishment of the Jerusalem Temple. Throughout his long reign he kept order in the land and gave Rome no cause to send in troops. But all of this came at a cost: Herod's home life was a disaster, not helped by his constant paranoia, and his subjects found his rule oppressive and tyrannical. When the old king died in 4 BCE, the land broke out in rebellion.

Herod had been given the unusual right to name his own successor, and the Roman Emperor Augustus upheld the king's final will, which had divided the land among three of his sons. Half of his territory, amounting to the regions of Judaea and Samaria, fell to Archaelaus; the north-eastern territories went to Philip; the remainder, comprising Galilee and Perea, to yet another son, Herod Antipas. Within a decade, however, Augustus was forced to reconsider. Archaelaus had proved to be a cruel ruler, and the emperor deposed him, bringing his territory under direct Roman rule. In 6 CE, Quirinius, the Legate of Syria, took a census to determine levels of taxation, and a Roman governor was sent out from Rome to administer the new province of Judaea. The governor – or 'prefect', to use his proper title – set up his provincial capital in the largely Gentile city of Caesarea on Sea, to the north west of the new province. His main concerns were the collection of taxes and the maintenance of law and order, for which he had a body of auxiliary troops. He was aided, however, by only a very small body of staff, and most of the day-to-day running of the province was devolved to the Jewish aristocracy in Jerusalem, with the High Priest at their head.

Growing up in Galilee, Jesus came under the jurisdiction of Antipas, whose long reign until 39 CE lent a certain stability to the region. Like his father before him, Antipas aspired to be a great builder, though his projects were far less grand in their ambition: he rebuilt the city of Sepphoris, which had been destroyed in the revolt after Herod's death, and founded a new administrative centre on the shores of the Sea of Galilee, naming it Tiberias in honour of the Emperor Tiberius. Antipas seems to have been a competent ruler; under him Galilee was reasonably stable, prosperous and peaceful. Most of his subjects worked the land: agricultural produce thrived in the mild climate and fertile soils, and most people reared livestock. Some were engaged in small industries, working in olive oil and wine production, the manufacture of pottery, the dyeing of wool, or in leather. The area around the Sea of Galilee was well known for fishing and its associated industries, including dried-fish production and boat building. Galileans themselves were largely rural folk, who spoke their native Aramaic with distinctive accents (Matthew 26.73) and may well have been more conservative in their outlook than their Judaean neighbours to the south.

Dreams, prophets and messiahs

Despite the relative calm, however, people harboured hopes of religious and national restoration. Ten of the twelve tribes of Israel had been wiped out in the Assyrian invasion in the eighth century BCE, and many dreamt of a future age of peace and prosperity when the twelve tribes of Israel would once again be restored and the land would be united under a messiah who ruled in God's name. Exactly what this messiah would be like was far from clear. Many envisaged a kingly figure, a second King David, who would rule over his people. Others imagined a priestly figure and still others pictured a future age without any messiah at all. There was clearly a deep-seated longing, a desire to return to the 'good old days', but for most people the hopes were vague and ill-defined.

Every now and then these hopes became more concrete. In 37 CE, a messiah appeared among the Samaritans, gathering a large crowd and promising to lead them up the sacred mountain of Gerizim, where he would show them certain holy vessels hidden there by Moses. The 40s saw two more prophetic leaders, this time in Judaea. A certain Theudas prepared to lead people to the River Jordan where – like Joshua of old – he would command the water to part and lead the people across. And a man known only as 'the Egyptian' persuaded a crowd of 30,000 people to follow him to the Mount of Olives, from where he planned to break into Jerusalem, overthrow the Roman garrison and seize the city. None of these movements came to anything: in every case, the Roman governor sent in his troops and stopped things in their tracks.

One of these prophetic figures has a particular bearing on our story: John the Baptist. John appeared at the River Jordan some time in the late 20s CE, calling people to repent of their ways and prepare themselves for God's judgement. In many respects he was the archetypal apocalyptic preacher, living a simple, frugal life and preaching his message of God's imminent arrival. As a sign of their repentance, John baptized his followers in the River Jordan. Ritual washing was common among Jews at the time, but what was distinctive about John's baptism was that it seems to have been intended as a one-off event, a symbolic outer cleansing of hearts and minds now ready to face the judgement of God. John was clearly extremely popular in his day, and the Jewish historian Josephus writes about him at some length, and with a certain amount of approval. The Gospels, too, suggest that large crowds went out to him in the desert, and that many presented themselves for baptism. Like the other prophetic figures mentioned above, however, John was executed, this time by Antipas, in whose territory he was active. But before he was imprisoned, one particular baptism was to prove especially significant.

Jesus' early life

We know virtually nothing of the first 30 years or so of Jesus' life. We shall see in the second part of this book that the stories associated with his birth are later, theological reflections. Tradition gives his father's name as Joseph, and the fact that he is not mentioned at all throughout Jesus' ministry has led to the reasonable assumption that he died relatively early. In Mark's Gospel, Jesus is known simply as the 'son of Mary', and he appears to have had four brothers and a number of sisters (Mark 6.3). The family home was in Nazareth, a rural village of around 400 people. Jesus' family had a trade: the Greek word used to describe them is *tektōn*, which means someone who works in wood or stone, broadly a carpenter or builder. Although not far up the social ladder, such a trade would allow the family to be economically self-sufficient.

Jesus seems to have grown up in a pious Jewish household. He would have been circumcised on the eighth day after birth, would have celebrated his bar-mitzvah at twelve and a half years old and attended synagogue on the Sabbath. Formal schooling was unknown in Galilean villages, and in a world where literacy levels were extremely low, it is unlikely Jesus had anything more than a basic ability in writing and arithmetic, perhaps only as much as he needed to practise his trade. But like other Jews, he would have acquired a deep knowledge of the Scriptures through their weekly recitation in the synagogue. The Gospels give the impression that he was a deeply spiritual man, someone who had reflected deeply on the traditions of his people and was ready to respond to God's call.

Not surprisingly, then, Jesus was attracted to the teachings of John the Baptist and offered himself for baptism; the slight unease the Gospels display at this event indirectly confirms its basis in fact (see especially Matthew 3.14–15). Something significant seems to have happened to Jesus at his baptism. The Gospels describe some sort of visionary experience: the heavens are torn apart; the Spirit descends as a dove; the voice of God declares Jesus to be his son. Whatever we make of the details, the scene suggests that Jesus had a powerful sense of being chosen by God, of being set aside for a specific task. Perhaps this was the first time that he understood himself to be God's envoy, a man with a mission of his own. Certainly his subsequent withdrawal into the wilderness, where he experienced a sense of testing by Satan, seems to confirm this interpretation. Only a few years later, the apostle Paul similarly took himself away to the desert after his experience on the Damascus road, to ponder what his new life might entail (Galatians 1.17). When Jesus emerged, it was with both a clear message and a sense of purpose.

3

Message and miracle

Central to Jesus' teaching was the imminent arrival of the kingdom of God. By this he meant *the direct rule of God over his people*, such that injustice and exploitation would disappear in the face of justice, mercy and peace. The Jewish Scriptures often imagine God as a king who chose Israel to be his special people, and the prophets frequently criticized the monarchy of their own day, looking forward to a time when God would once again establish his reign. Like the prophet Isaiah, Jesus saw a kingdom where the blind would see, the deaf hear, the lame leap, the dumb sing and all creation become fertile (Isaiah 35 – a passage that may well have provided a blueprint for Jesus' own vision).

But when would this kingdom be established? There is much in Jesus' teaching to suggest that, like John before him, Jesus imagined that God would appear in the near future, heralding a time of cosmic judgement and world transformation. Several of Jesus' parables urge his followers to keep watch for the hour of judgement, and certain sayings clearly expect the future arrival of God's reign (see especially Mark 9.1; 10.23; 13.30). And yet at the same time some of Jesus' sayings suggest that the kingdom is already present within the community of believers. Parables such as the mustard seed (Mark 4.30–32) give the impression that the kingdom is here already, unnoticed and growing quietly. Perhaps both strands need to be held in tension. On the one hand, Jesus sees the kingdom so clearly that there is a sense in which it is already coming into being through his words and actions – particularly the miracles, which we shall look at in a moment. On the other hand, there will still be a final, future consummation of God's reign.

In order to prepare for the kingdom, Jesus asked his followers to repent of their ways. What he demanded, in effect, was that people radically reorientate their lives towards God, a reorientation that would result in ethical behaviour. Much of Jesus' ethical teaching is found in Matthew's Sermon on the Mount (Matthew 5—7; a similar collection is found in Luke 6). This material is generally thought to derive from the 'Q' source (see pp. 7–8), and even if we cannot be sure Jesus spoke these exact words, it is likely that they represent the kind of things he was remembered to have said. Many of his most quoted and loved sayings belong to this material: the command to love one's enemies and pray for persecutors (Matthew 5.44//Luke 6.28, 35); to give alms and fast in secret (Matthew 6.4, 17–18); not to serve God and Mammon (Matthew 6.24//Luke 16.13); not to judge others (Matthew 7.1–2//Luke 6.37–38). We might call this an *interim ethic*, showing people how to prepare themselves and live in readiness for the final consummation of all things. Jesus' teaching is neatly summed up by the Lord's Prayer, which combines both future hopes and present ethical expectations:

> Our Father in heaven,
> hallowed be your name.
> Your kingdom come,
> your will be done,
> on earth as it is in heaven.

Give us this day our daily bread,
and forgive us our debts,
as we also have forgiven our debtors.
And lead us not into temptation, but deliver us from
 evil.   (Matthew 6.9–13; compare the shorter
                                version in Luke 11.2–4)

Jesus was clearly a gifted teacher, a charismatic personality and a good communicator. He expressed himself through witty sayings, proverbs and parables, all drawn from the realities of peasant life in first-century Galilee. And undergirding it all was a strong personal sense that the God who would reign as king could also be experienced in the most intimate way, as father.

Miracles

Closely associated with Jesus' message were his extraordinary powers. According to the Gospels, he had amazing abilities both to heal the sick and drive out unclean spirits from those who flocked to him. It is worth remembering that ordinary people in the ancient world had very little access to medical help. What doctors there were largely worked among the city elite, charging for their services; peasant folk in rural Galilee would have had little chance ever to meet such men. Some people were skilled in herbal remedies, such as the Essenes, who wrote the Dead Sea Scrolls, and midwives might offer some degree of help to birthing mothers. Most of the time, however, illness went untreated. We can easily imagine the excitement created by someone reputed to be skilled in the arts of healing, and it is no surprise to find Jesus surrounded by expectant crowds – some wanting healing themselves, others gathering no doubt to witness a great spectacle. It was probably Jesus' extraordinary abilities rather than his preaching that first rallied the crowds.

To many modern people, these miraculous events are the hardest part of the Gospel tradition to accept. We live in a scientific world where we expect to be able to explain most things – particularly in the medical sphere. In many respects, however, it is not the historian's task to ask whether these events actually happened; we have no way of knowing whether what we understand as the usual rules of nature were temporarily suspended. All the historian can do is note that people around Jesus seem to have thought he had amazing abilities. Nor was Jesus unique in the ancient world in this respect. Acts of healing were often credited to certain gods – specifically Asclepius, the god of healing, whose temples are littered with notes of thanks from cured supplicants. Two Jewish holy men, Honi the Circle-Drawer and Hanina ben Dosa, who lived around the same time as Jesus, were both credited with spectacular feats: Honi provided rain at a time of drought; Hanina is said to have been able to heal sickness, stop a deluge and even miraculously lengthen pieces of wood. Emperors and great men were also popularly held to have miraculous powers: the first-century Jewish writer Philo of Alexandria credits the Emperor Augustus with stilling the seas and healing disease.[3]

The Jewish historian Josephus credits Jesus with 'surprising feats'. We saw in Chapter 1 that this particular paragraph is suspect, but the sentence in which this phrase occurs is generally taken to be genuine. As such it provides non-Christian evidence to suggest that Jesus was popularly regarded as a doer of miraculous works. It is interesting that opponents of Jesus counter his miracles not by claiming that they have not happened but by accusing him of being in league with satanic powers. In Mark 3.22, for example, the scribes from Jerusalem accuse Jesus of casting out demons by the power of Beelzebul, the prince of demons. The point at issue is not whether miraculous healings and exorcisms happened, but by whose power. A couple of centuries later, this charge would surface again in rabbinic literature, where Jesus was accused of being a sorcerer; that is, of conjuring up evil powers in his service. Followers claimed that Jesus acted through the power of God, opponents that he acted through satanic forces.

The significance of Jesus' miracles is that they show the kingdom of God breaking into people's lives, giving a glimpse of a future world in which the lame can truly walk, the blind see, the deaf hear and evil spirits are cast out. There is a sense of restoring the afflicted, bringing them back to wholeness and reintegrating the outcast into society. This is particularly evident in the case of lepers, who would have been excluded from everyday life and shunned by everyone they met. By curing a leper, Jesus did more than heal him from a life-threatening disease; he reintegrated him into the community, an act that underlined the inclusivity of the kingdom. Thus message and miracle were closely linked to Jesus' vision of the future reign of God.

Political implications

So far we have explored the religious dimension of Jesus' message. But in the first century, religion and politics were integrally intertwined. Jesus' proclamation of the coming kingdom also included highly subversive political overtones that would not have been lost on his contemporaries. Talk of a kingdom, even God's kingdom, had clear nationalistic dimensions. Even if Jesus was not calling his followers to arms, his message had clear political implications.

When the Jewish Scriptures talk of God's future reign, they often imagine the gathering together of the scattered people of Israel. That Jesus also expected the restitution of the twelve tribes is shown by his decision to surround himself with twelve male disciples. Strangely, perhaps, the lists in the Gospels of who made up the twelve are not in exact agreement (compare Mark 13.17–1 with Matthew 10.2–4 and Luke 6.14–16). This suggests that the *symbolic value* of 'the twelve' was more significant than the precise identity of every member. A passage found in both Matthew and Luke, and generally held to be part of their common source, 'Q', makes the identification of the disciples with the twelve tribes clear:

> Jesus said to them [the disciples], 'Truly, I say to you, in the new world, when the Son of man will sit on his glorious throne, you who have followed me will also sit on twelve thrones, judging the twelve tribes of Israel.'
>
> (Matthew 19.28; see also Luke 22.30)

Jesus' message was clear: Israel would be whole again, as in the great days of David and Solomon; Rome and all earthly governments would be swept away; God would establish his reign for ever. This potent cluster of ideas tapped into some of the most strongly held hopes of his Jewish contemporaries, but it was dangerously subversive to those in power.

4

Friends, enemies – and a wife?

In the earliest phase of his ministry, Jesus based himself in Capernaum, a thriving fishing village on the north-west shore of the Sea of Galilee. Yet right from the start he travelled around the local towns and settlements, taking his message out to as wide an audience as possible. Rather than wait for people to find him, he sought out new audiences, confronting them with his urgent message of the approaching kingdom. Everywhere he went, large crowds gathered, some because they hoped to be healed, some for religious or political reasons and others no doubt simply to be part of something new and exciting. Opinions regarding Jesus varied: some held him to be a prophet, perhaps like John the Baptist or one of the Israelite prophets of old; others began to question whether he might be something more, perhaps even the longed-for Messiah.

Things, however, seem to have been less good at home. We shall see later that Matthew and Luke both suggest that Jesus' family knew from his conception that he was God's chosen one, destined for a special role. But Mark's Gospel knows nothing of this. In fact his brief references to Jesus' family suggest that Jesus' mission was a cause of tension. In Mark 3.20–21, Jesus' family come to take him home because people were saying he was crazy. Ignoring them, Jesus told the assembled crowd that his true mother and siblings were not his biological family but those who believed his words.

Later on, when he returned to his home town of Nazareth, there is no suggestion either that Jesus went back to his family home or even that they stood up for him in the face of local opposition. And while John places Jesus' mother at the cross, there is no record of her presence in Mark or Luke or Matthew, who base their accounts on Mark. There is not much to go on here, but there is enough to suppose that the common assumption that Jesus' family supported his mission is misplaced. In many respects, tension might be easily explained: if Jesus were the eldest, and if his father had died, he would be expected to take his place at the head of the family, running the family business, arranging his sisters' weddings and providing for his mother and younger siblings. It might well have appeared to his family that he was ignoring his responsibilities.

Who, then, did Jesus regard as his extended family? We have seen already that he chose twelve men as his closest followers, and that they had a special symbolic place in his movement. It is clear, however, that these were not Jesus' only disciples, nor were they the only ones to journey around Galilee with him. Mark mentions Galilean women who travelled with Jesus (15.40–41), and Luke names them as Mary Magdalene, Joanna the wife of Herod's steward Chuza – perhaps therefore a woman of some importance – and an otherwise unknown Salome. Clearly the presence of women did not raise any eyebrows; at any rate no criticism is recorded in the Gospels. Perhaps the group was large enough not to occasion comment, and in any case similar mixed groups would have frequently travelled to Jerusalem on pilgrimage – in Luke 2 we get a sense of a large pilgrimage company in the story of the twelve-year-old Jesus left behind in Jerusalem. Luke suggests that the women offered financial aid to the movement, perhaps stepping in when hospitality was unavailable, buying provisions and overseeing some of the practicalities of life on the road. Of course, none of this would preclude a personal commitment to Jesus and his message, nor should we suppose that the women were any less 'disciples' than their male counterparts. Millenarian movements that looked forward to the transformation of society were often egalitarian, and Jesus seems to have been as welcoming of women as he was of men. But did one of these women have a particularly close relationship to him?

Was Jesus married?

In popular culture it is frequently claimed that Jesus was married to Mary Magdalene. There are two stages to this argument. The first is to claim that marriage and procreation were sacred duties for first-century Jews, and that Jesus would have been highly unusual if he were not married. The second is to point to certain later, gnostic texts in which Mary features prominently. This prominence, it is argued, is a later memory of a much closer relation between them.

Neither of these arguments holds any weight. First, it might well be that most Jews saw marriage as a sacred obligation, but this hardly means that every male Jew was married. A man with a particular interest in religious matters could easily have chosen to remain single and to devote himself to the service of his God. Those who took themselves into the desert at Qumran relinquished married life; there is no evidence that John the Baptist was married; and the apostle Paul specifically says that he was unmarried (1 Corinthians 7.8). Singleness, though unusual, was not unheard of, and might even be expected in one who thought that the world as he knew it was about to be swept away with the arrival of God.

Second, it is worth noting how seldom Mary Magdalene is mentioned in the Gospels. Mark mentions her only at the end of his narrative, noting that she was among a group of women who had followed Jesus from Galilee. These women play an important role in the Gospel as the link between the crucifixion, the burial and the empty tomb on the Sunday morning, but otherwise Mark has no further interest in any of them. Luke adds a note that Jesus cast out seven demons from Mary (Luke 8.2), while John claims that she was the first to see the risen Jesus (John 20). The portrait that emerges is of someone who was healed by Jesus and responded by leaving her home and devoting her life to following him. We have no idea how old she was – she could have been a young woman, as she is consistently portrayed in films, but she might just as easily have been an older widow, which might explain why she had independent means and the ability to go where she liked.

Mary becomes much more prominent in certain gnostic gospels, which date from the second century onwards (see pp. 55–7). In a number of these texts, Mary is said to have a particularly close relationship with Jesus: the *Gospel of Mary* claims that Jesus loved her more than any of his other followers, while the *Gospel of Philip* presents her as Jesus' 'companion', and she frequently arouses the jealousy of other disciples, especially Peter. The difficulty lies in knowing what to do with these highly esoteric texts, which show very little interest in the historical Jesus. It would certainly be a mistake to assume that they reflect a historical reminiscence that Mary was married to Jesus. In all likelihood they are theological developments drawn from John's account of her speaking with the risen Jesus, perhaps reflecting the – rather ambiguous – place of women within the contemporary gnostic churches.[4]

Before we leave Mary Magdalene, it is also worth pointing out that there is no evidence to suggest that she was a repentant prostitute. This view, first promoted by Pope Gregory the Great in the sixth century, comes from combining a number of New Testament texts. Most important here is the story of Jesus' anointing by a woman shortly before his death. In John's Gospel it is Mary of Bethany who anoints him (12.1–8), while the other Gospels do not name her. Luke tells a similar story much earlier, while Jesus is still in Galilee, and the anointing is performed by a 'woman from the city', 'a sinner' (Luke 7.36–50). While this description is hardly explicit, it has traditionally been taken as evidence that Mary was a prostitute. Furthermore, the unknown woman taken in adultery (John 8.1–11) has also been grafted on to this composite portrait, to produce the characteristic image of Mary Magdalene. Her decision to follow Jesus after he expelled her 'demons' completes the traditional portrait of the repentant prostitute. Clearly this characterization of Mary has no historical basis – and it was never accepted by the Eastern Orthodox churches – but the stress on penitence within medieval theology meant that the image endured well into the modern period, enhanced by centuries of paintings, sculptures and, more recently, novels and films (see p. 76).

Pharisees

Jesus was a controversial figure, and while many flocked to him, others regarded him with suspicion and distrust.

Most prominent here were the Pharisees, though we need to use our sources cautiously at this point. All four Gospels were written in the late first century, at a time when Christ-followers were engaged in heated debate with their Jewish neighbours in the synagogues. It is likely that the Gospels reflect the turbulent 'parting of the ways' between the two faiths, and that the Pharisees in particular, as representatives of Jewish opponents, are portrayed in a hostile manner, characterized as self-satisfied hypocrites who want to do away with Jesus (Mark 3.6).

In reality the Pharisees were well liked and respected by ordinary folk. They were a group of pious Jews who aimed to adhere as closely as possible to both the written law – as laid down in the Jewish Scriptures – and also their own oral traditions. Central to Pharisaism was the accurate interpretation of Scripture, and they engaged in often heated debates with both opponents and one another over matters of purity, Sabbath observance, food laws and the like. They were particularly interested in purity, and tended to separate themselves from other people, aiming to keep themselves in the same state of purity that was required of priests in the Temple. With a new preacher in town, it was inevitable that the Pharisees would seek him out and challenge his opinions.

In many respects Jesus had much in common with the Pharisees. It is important to note that there is never any question of Jesus *breaking* the Jewish law; all indications suggest that he was law-observant, even if some of his interpretations might have been a little unorthodox. The Pharisees would have agreed with him on the centrality of love and concern for one's neighbour; few would have disputed that it is what comes out of a person that makes her pure or impure (Mark 7.15); and few would have objected to Jesus' healing on the Sabbath by word alone. What seems to have particularly riled the Pharisees was Jesus' determination to eat with outcasts, tax-collectors and sinners (Mark 2.15–17). Who a person ate with in the ancient world, as today, had important social and cultural implications. For Jesus, shared meals with repentant undesirables functioned as symbolic enactments of the 'messianic banquet', a great feast associated with the end times in the Jewish Scriptures. Shared table-fellowship showed that forgiveness was available for all, even those considered 'sinners' by the more pious, and once again highlighted the inclusive nature of the kingdom. From the Pharisees' perspective, however, such meals only underscored Jesus' naivety: what was the point of living a righteous life if tax-collectors and sinners were to be the first in the kingdom of God? Why should anyone believe in their repentance? And could a man who promoted such undesirables really claim to speak for God?

Jesus was happy to engage in debate with the Pharisees, countering their criticisms with scriptural quotations and arguments of his own. But there was another threat in Galilee which Jesus seemed far less inclined to engage with: Herod Antipas. The Jewish ruler had of course killed John the Baptist around the start of Jesus' ministry, and the Gospels suggest that some of his courtiers were attracted to the new movement (Luke 8.2–3) and that Antipas had himself already started to take an interest in the new preacher (Mark 6.14–16). A curious feature of the record in the Gospels is that there is never any suggestion that Jesus went to either of Galilee's two cities. This is particularly surprising given that Sepphoris is visible from Nazareth, only an hour's walk away, and Tiberias is located on the Sea of

Galilee, close to Jesus' other haunts. Both cities were centres of local government and bureaucracy in the region, and while still largely Jewish, would have afforded Jesus a wealthier, more cosmopolitan audience for his message. But the cities were also the heart of Antipas' power, and it may be that Jesus deliberately avoided them in an attempt not to attract his attention. Anyone who attracted large crowds and stirred up the hopes of the people with talk of another kingdom was unlikely to have survived long in Antipas' territory.

At some point in his ministry Jesus left Galilee and went to Jerusalem, 100 miles to the south. The great cosmopolitan city was the traditional capital of Israel, the site of God's Temple and was believed by Jews to be the holiest place on earth. Several prophetic visions in the Jewish Scriptures expected the city to play a prominent role in the end times (see Isaiah 60—62; Ezekiel 40—48), so it is not surprising to find Jesus taking his message there. Perhaps he too expected that God could appear in judgement nowhere other than in Jerusalem.

5

Jerusalem, betrayal and execution

We have no idea how many times Jesus went to the capital city, nor even how long his ministry lasted. Mark's chronology, which is followed by Matthew and Luke, gives the impression that the ministry lasted for no more than a year, with only one visit to Jerusalem. But Mark gives a highly stylized account, grouping all the Galilean material in the first half of the book and all the Jerusalem material in the second. This arrangement can tell us nothing about the actual chronology of Jesus' ministry. John's Gospel gives a different impression. There Jesus goes to Jerusalem to celebrate several Jewish feasts in the course of a ministry that lasts at least two and a half years. But again we need to be cautious. John wants to present Jesus as the replacement of Jewish feasts, and this is done most effectively by bringing him to the holy city at various festal settings, so that Jesus can be seen as the light of the world at Hanukkah – a feast celebrated through light – or the true paschal lamb at Passover. Again, overhasty reliance on John were best avoided. It seems, then, that we cannot be sure how long Jesus' ministry lasted, nor how many times he visited Jerusalem. As a pious Jew, it might be expected that he would have made the pilgrimage to the holy city as often as he could, and it is quite possible that he and the disciples visited it on a number of occasions. What concerns us below, however, is his last, fatal visit.

The Gospels associate a number of key events with this last Jerusalem visit: a symbolic entry into Jerusalem; an incident in the Temple (though John locates this earlier in the ministry); Jesus' betrayal by a close friend; a symbolic meal; Jesus' arrest, trial and execution. We need to look at each of these in turn, but first it is crucial to appreciate the significance of the Passover setting. The feast celebrated the exodus from Egypt and liberation from bondage and foreign oppression. It was one of the three great pilgrimage celebrations, and Jerusalem and the surrounding area would have been crowded to bursting. The festivities lasted around a week, but most people came a week earlier to purify themselves. It would have been a time of great national celebration, of families reuniting, and a carnival atmosphere prevailed. But it was also a time when political hopes and messianic dreams might be at their height and trouble was likely to break out. Indeed, Josephus notes that most riots took place at Passover, and it was for this reason that the Roman governor came to the city with a body of troops, to make sure he was on hand if trouble broke out. It was into this highly charged situation that Jesus arrived with his disciples.

Entry into Jerusalem and an incident in the Temple

Jesus is said to have made his last journey into Jerusalem on the back of a donkey. To us this conjures up images of lowliness and humility, but this is to misinterpret the significance of the scene. In the ancient world, donkeys were the usual means of transport; it was on a donkey that Joshua and his sons judged Israel, and on a donkey that Solomon

31

rode to his coronation. The point of the story is that while all the other pilgrims made their way into the city on foot, Jesus rode in to the cheers of the crowds. This was clearly a statement: in effect what Jesus did was to enter the city in triumph, announcing himself as God's envoy.

The next day he entered the Temple and acted equally provocatively. According to the Gospels, he went into the outer court and overturned the tables of the money changers and pigeon sellers. Scholars have long debated the meaning of this incident. It clearly could not have been a huge event: the outer court of the Temple was immense – the size of twelve football pitches – and any demonstration by one man alone could only have been fairly small-scale. Besides, the Temple police do not seem to have arrested him on the spot, which they surely would have done if the demonstration had lasted more than a few minutes. It is probably best to see it as a prophetic act, rather like those performed by the Old Testament prophets. For example, Jeremiah wore a yoke around his neck to symbolize the impending Babylonian victory; Isaiah went naked and barefoot for three years as a sign against Egypt and Ethiopia; Ezekiel took on himself the punishment of Israel by lying on his side for 390 days. Jesus' outburst, then, was designed to symbolize something – but what?

We can discount immediately any suggestion that Jesus set himself against the sacrificial system. Eventually, of course, once the Temple had fallen to the Romans, Christianity – and Judaism – dispensed with the Temple and sacrifice. But in the ancient world, to sacrifice was to worship. The offerings in the Temple were all demanded by God, and we should guard against interpreting the first century in the light of our own modern prejudices. Problematic too is the common assumption that Jesus was protesting against corruption among the high priestly aristocracy. It is often claimed that the Temple priests enjoyed a monopoly on the sale of sacrificial animals, and that they used weighted measures in their financial transactions. This is clearly possible, though there is no ancient evidence that the priestly aristocracy were generally seen as corrupt, nor does such a charge feature in Jesus' teaching elsewhere.

It is more likely, in the view of most scholars, that Jesus' demonstration signified *the destruction of the Temple*. This explanation has the advantage of fitting well into Jesus' overarching message. Elsewhere he envisages a time when the Temple will no longer stand (see Mark 13.2 in particular), and the overturning of the tables was a graphic symbol of the destruction to come. Like other apocalyptic prophets, Jesus seems to have imagined that God would come and destroy the earthly Temple, perhaps replacing it with a heavenly one. In any event, Jesus' actions were a direct challenge to people's complacency: God's arrival was imminent, and the Temple would be destroyed.

Although small-scale, both the triumphal entry and the Temple incident would have alarmed the Jewish authorities. We have already seen that Rome left the general running of the city in the hands of the priestly aristocrats, with the Roman-appointed High Priest at the head. By the time of Jesus, the office was occupied by a man called Joseph Caiaphas. He had been appointed in 19 CE by Pilate's predecessor, Gratus, and was presumably from Rome's point of view a capable politician and a safe pair of hands – if not, he would have been quickly replaced. Rome expected these native authorities to be shrewd enough to keep the peace, to act as intermediaries between the interests of Rome and the native population, and to intervene only when riots broke out. Presumably Caiaphas and his entourage would have been watching Jesus for some time – reports would probably have reached them even while he was in Galilee, and they would have been prepared for his arrival. With Jesus in Jerusalem, however, the situation had become dangerous: he had a following, his teaching might incite the crowds to riot, and he had brought it all to the most holy place. As far as the chief priests were concerned, the smooth running of the Temple over the Passover was paramount. Jesus had already brought his message into the Temple, and who knew what he might do next. If his actions brought Roman troops into the Temple, it would mean the pollution and defilement of the sacred place, as well as bloodshed. All in all it was better to remove Jesus before he caused any more trouble.

Jesus' betrayal

But how was Jesus to be removed? The Gospels suggest that the chief priests enlisted one of Jesus' followers, Judas Iscariot. The embarrassment of admitting that one of Jesus' closest friends betrayed him has convinced most scholars that this is a historically reliable detail. Why, though, did Judas do it? The Gospels give us very little information on this point. Matthew implies that Judas was motivated by greed, though 30 pieces of silver, the price of a slave, was a paltry sum and would not have kept Judas more than a month or so. Luke and John can only assume that Judas was possessed by Satan. Modern scholars have been even more creative in their explanations. Some suggest that he became disillusioned by Jesus, perhaps hoping that his ministry might have taken a more political course. Others have argued that Judas wanted to force Jesus' hand, engineering a meeting with the High Priest in the expectation that things would come to a head. Others still have suggested that Jesus himself was behind Judas' actions, that he put Judas up to it – though this perhaps smacks of later attempts to take away the stigma of Jesus' betrayal by a close friend. Of all the disciples, Judas is the only one who may not have been a Galilean: his name meant 'man from Kerioth', a settlement in Judaea. We might speculate that Judas felt estranged from the rest of the group, or that the Temple priests used their local networks to get to him in some way. In the end, however, we cannot know what drove Judas to betray his master. What he betrayed was not so much the content of Jesus' teaching but Jesus' physical location, by suggesting a time when he could be apprehended with a minimum of fuss.

A symbolic last meal

Jesus spent his last evening with his friends in a borrowed room in Jerusalem. There is no reason to suppose that the group comprised only the twelve male disciples, as Leonardo da Vinci's famous late fifteenth-century mural implies. Presumably the gathering included the women who had travelled with Jesus from Galilee, as well as other close friends and supporters. In all probability Jesus realized that his death might well be imminent. Even if he had no inkling of Judas' treachery, he had seen the fate of John the Baptist and knew that his own behaviour since he came to Jerusalem had been provocative. Perhaps he took the opportunity to prepare his disciples for a future without him, when they themselves would carry on his work. Or perhaps, emboldened by the Passover commemoration of God's saving acts in the past, he hoped God would intervene in the nick of time, snatching him from death and establishing his kingdom.

Jesus' words at this gathering are some of the most famous he ever uttered, and have been repeated at the Christian Eucharist ever since. We actually have a number of different versions: one in Mark; an almost identical one in Matthew; a rather different one in Luke that features two cups; one in a second-century Christian manual known as the *Didache* with quite different words. All of these no doubt reflect the words used by their authors' own Christian groups. The oldest report, however, is preserved in one of Paul's letters, and dates to within 20 years of Jesus' death:

> the Lord Jesus on the night when he was betrayed took bread, and when he had given thanks, he broke it, and said, 'This is my body which is for you. Do this in remembrance of me.' In the same way also he took the cup, after supper, saying, 'This cup is the new covenant in my blood. Do this, as often as you drink it, in remembrance of me.'
>
> (1 Corinthians 11.23–25)

No doubt Jesus' words quickly achieved an important symbolic status as his followers reflected on their last gathering. The bread and the wine would become symbols of Jesus' broken body; Jesus' death was seen as a new covenant with God; the Last Supper itself was understood as a Christian ritual to be repeated regularly until Jesus' return in glory. How much – if any – of this goes back to the historical Jesus and how much to the reflection of the early Church is difficult to say. In any event it is unlikely that Jesus was

surprised when the Temple police came to arrest him later
that evening.

Jesus' arrest, trial and execution

The question of whether Jesus had a formal Jewish trial
has been one of the most controversial in historical Jesus
studies, particularly since the Second World War and the
greater sensitivity in recent decades towards the anti-Jewish
bias of several New Testament texts. Our accounts of Jesus'
last few hours differ quite considerably. Mark, followed
by Matthew, records a formal night-time trial in front of
a Jewish council, with witnesses, charges and a verdict.
Luke presents a scaled-down version the following morning, which merely forms the preliminary to handing Jesus
over to Rome. And John includes only a brief hearing in
front of Annas, a former High Priest and the father-in-law
of Caiaphas. Where they agree is the implicit claim that the
prime movers against Jesus were the Jewish authorities, and
that the Roman governor was reluctant to pass sentence –
Luke even suggests that Pilate tried to release the prisoner
three times.

Modern scholars are convinced that this tendentious
portrait derives from the historical setting of the earliest
Christians. As far as they were concerned, Jews had rejected
the message of Jesus, and the new mission grounds would
be found in the Roman world, particularly in the large
cities around the Mediterranean. The main difficulty
facing Christian missionaries, however, was the crucifixion.
Romans might be attracted to the teachings of Jesus, but
persuading them to put their faith in a teacher who had
been sentenced to a shameful death by a Roman governor

was no easy task. The strategy they alighted on was to stress the involvement of Jewish authorities in Jesus' death and minimize the role played by Rome. The rhetorical pay-off was clear: Roman converts need not worry that they were joining a subversive group, Jesus' execution was down to the machinations of jealous Jewish authorities and he himself was guiltless under Roman law.

Reconstructing historical events from such explosive material is no easy task. Some would deny any Jewish involvement in Jesus' arrest, arguing that crucifixion was a Roman penalty and that someone of Jesus' lowly status could easily have been taken out and executed straight after the incident in the Temple. Others put forward a more moderate view, which acknowledges *some* involvement by the Jewish leaders but assigns to them a much less crucial role than in the Gospels. We have already seen that the High Priest and the Jerusalem aristocracy worked closely with Rome. Their imperial overlords expected them to uphold Roman interests and to smoothe over tensions; in the pursuit of peace, they probably had little choice but to comply. No doubt the priestly leaders watched Jesus with growing concern and conveyed their anxieties to the Roman prefect. But anyone the chief priests were worried about was undoubtedly a concern to Pilate too. It is hardly likely that the first time he heard of Jesus was when the chief priests had him arrested. Pilate would have had a network of spies and informers, including men of the highest rank, such as Antipas, who would have kept him appraised of Jesus' activities even before he arrived in Jerusalem. Presumably he would have needed very little persuading that Jesus was a threat to security and needed to be eliminated quickly.

It is worth emphasizing once again the shameful nature of crucifixion. The punishment was considered too demeaning for Roman citizens and could be inflicted only on people of low status, robbers, bandits and slaves. Victims were naked (the loincloth in depictions of the crucifixion is a nod to Christian modesty), frequently abused by the Roman guards and held up as a spectacle for the contempt and derision of the gathered crowds. Crucifixion was designed as a deterrent, and a statement of the charge against the prisoner was usually attached to the cross. If Jesus' charge read 'King of the Jews', as the Gospels suggest, then it was probably intended to mock any messianic claims that Jesus – or his followers – might have entertained.

Mark suggests that Jesus died with a cry of abandonment: 'My God, my God, why have you forsaken me?' This is a quotation from Psalm 22, which colours the whole of Mark's account of the crucifixion. We cannot know for sure, but it is quite probable that one who lived his life according to the Scriptures should die with these words on his lips. Perhaps he drew strength, encouragement and even hope from words popularly believed to come from none other than King David in his darkest hour. Rather more romantically, Luke has Jesus die forgiving his enemies and committing his spirit to the Father (Luke 23.34, 46), and the Johannine Jesus dies in triumphal completion of his work (John 19.30).

Victims of crucifixion were not usually granted any kind of burial; the corpse would simply rot, becoming carrion for the birds and the dogs. Not to be buried was considered deeply shameful in the ancient world, a complete annihilation of one's whole identity. The Gospels, of course, insist that Jesus *was* buried, that a Jewish aristocrat by the name of Joseph of Arimathea intervened on his behalf and gave him a decent, if hurried, interment. But is this likely? There is archaeological evidence that at least one crucified man was released to his family for burial. The remains of a 20-year-old man named Yehohanan were found in 1968 with the iron nail still through the ankle bone; presumably those who buried him were unable to remove it after they lifted him down from the cross. And it is easy to imagine a social context in which the Roman prefect might have allowed the body of a relatively harmless preacher to be buried rather than hang in disgrace throughout the Passover festival. But if Jesus was buried, it was likely a shameful interment in a pauper's grave rather than the respectable tomb envisaged by the Evangelists. And rather than a secret friend, Joseph of Arimathea was more likely the councillor charged with the unpleasant task of overseeing the disposal of the bodies of those deemed to be criminals by the state.

*   *   *

So ended the life of Jesus of Nazareth. It would be wrong to see Jesus as the 'first Christian' – like all of his earliest followers, he lived and died as a Jew. Nor is it at all likely that Jesus saw himself as establishing a new religion – he longed for the renewal of Israel and the establishment of the reign of God, not a new faith. Ordinarily he would have been forgotten, little more than a mention in the pages of contemporary chroniclers, but something totally unexpected took place. Within days of his execution, Jesus' followers were gripped by a profound sense that he had been raised from the dead and exalted to the right hand of God. With this claim, the focus of the movement was no longer solely on his teaching but on his identity – as the one raised by God to glory. And gradually, Jesus would be depicted in ever more exalted terms as the movement that gathered in his name grew from a small group in a backwater province to become the world's largest religion. In Part 2 we shall consider Jesus' immense legacy, starting with the event that sparked it all: the belief that Jesus had been raised from the dead.

Part 2

JESUS' LEGACY

6

From Jewish prophet
to Gentile God

According to the Gospels, it all started with an empty grave. When a group of women went back to the place where Jesus was buried a couple of days after the crucifixion, the body was no longer there. The apostle Paul, writing perhaps 20 years earlier, doesn't mention an empty tomb but instead records a number of resurrection appearances, including one to himself on the Damascus road (1 Corinthians 15.3–8). Whether the tomb was in fact empty is something the historian cannot answer definitively. It is also important to note that an empty tomb on its own would not normally lead anyone to suspect that the body had been raised from the dead. A host of more likely explanations would come to mind: that the women had gone to the wrong grave, that the body had been stolen, that someone had moved it, and so on. Nevertheless, it is clear from the ancient sources that soon after his death, Jesus' followers were filled with an overpowering sense that God had raised him from the dead. So intense was this conviction that it turned them from frightened disciples into bold missionaries willing to die for their faith.

The resurrection convinced Jesus' earliest followers that the end of the world had come. Although that sounds odd to us, it was a natural inference to draw. Most Jews believed there would be a general resurrection at the end of time, when God would come in judgement. If Jesus had been raised from the dead, it could mean only one thing: that the end time had dawned and that others would soon be raised to glory too. This of course meshed well with Jesus' own message, in which he announced the impending arrival of God, and explains the urgency with which Christian missionaries set about preaching the message around the eastern Mediterranean.

From the very earliest times, Jesus' followers tried to explain his role in God's plan for the world and to make sense of his death and resurrection. As Jews, the obvious place to search for meaning was within their sacred Scriptures. This collection of ancient texts told the history of Israel but was also believed to declare God's will in the present. When approached in this way, many texts could be seen as pointing to Jesus, particularly certain psalms and passages from the prophets. Followers began to see Jesus as the fulfilment of biblical texts, to describe him in ever more exalted terms and to transform the humiliation of the cross into something filled with theological significance.

St Paul

The most significant figure in this early period was the apostle Paul. Trained as a Pharisee, Paul seems at first to have been violently opposed to the new faith, even going so far as to persecute believers. An unexpected and dramatic vision of the risen Jesus on the road to Damascus, however, caused him to stop in his tracks and, after some reflection and soul-searching, to redirect the rest of his life to following Christ (for a fascinating first-hand account of this, see Galatians 1.11–24).

Paul was tireless in spreading the message to new regions, founding churches all over the eastern Mediterranean and keeping in touch with them by letter. The New Testament contains 13 letters by Paul, though modern scholars question the genuineness of some. The real importance of Paul for our story is that he provides such an early written record of Christian speculation about Jesus. He puts great theological weight on the cross and resurrection, seeing them as the basis of human salvation and the start of a new age (see 2 Corinthians 5.15–17 and Galatians 6.14–15). For the great apostle, the death of Jesus eclipses the whole of his early life and forms the basis of his followers' identity and outlook.

Paul takes it for granted that Jesus is the Messiah of Jewish expectation, though it is a radically transformed messiahship, which now incorporates the idea of suffering. He sees Jesus as the prototype of a new humanity, a second Adam. Just as the first Adam brought sin, death and universal condemnation into the world through his disobedience, so Jesus brought righteousness, life and acquittal to all people through his obedience to the Father's will. Paul talks of Jesus as God's son, but in certain passages blurs the distinction between the two (an example here is Philippians 2.9–11). In all of this he is probably simply reflecting views current within his contemporary Church. What is remarkable, however, is the degree of theological speculation that had built up around Jesus within no more than a decade or two of his death. For monotheistic Jews even to countenance such a close connection between Jesus and God is striking indeed.

Where Paul was more of an innovator was in the matter of extending the mission to non-Jews (otherwise known as Gentiles). This difficulty had not presented itself during Jesus' ministry when all of the first converts had been Jews. But gradually it became more of an issue. Could non-Jews become followers of Christ? All were agreed that they could, but on what basis? Most were of the opinion that they first had to become Jews; that is, to be circumcised in the case of men, and to keep the Jewish law. This would have seemed like an eminently sensible solution to most people: it meant that all Christ-followers kept the law and that there were no problems with table-fellowship or other joint gatherings. Paul, however, was violently opposed to this way of reasoning. For him, what God had done through the resurrection of Jesus was to open up a completely new way for people to achieve salvation. All anyone had to do was to believe in what God had done. To ask people to do anything on top of this – in effect, to ask non-Jews to keep the Jewish law – was to downplay God's decisive actions through the cross and resurrection of Jesus. In the end, Paul's arguments were accepted, and Gentiles were welcomed into the new faith without being required to keep the law.

Many have credited Paul with being the real founder of Christianity, arguing that it was he who turned a Jewish sect into a universal religion. This is probably going too far, but he was certainly one of the Church's greatest thinkers, and he can be credited with putting the law-free mission to the Gentiles on a firm theoretical basis. If new converts had been required to keep the Jewish law, that would undoubtedly have dampened the appeal of the new faith within the late first-century Roman world. Luke tells us that already by the 50s CE, a large community of Christ-followers had gathered in the Syrian city of Antioch and that it was here they were first known as 'Christians'. From now on Christianity had the means to spread throughout the Roman Empire.

The first Gospels

If Paul gave a theological underpinning to the expanding Church, it was the Gospels that provided the first biographies of its founding figure, starting with Mark in the early 70s CE. By this time, many of the first generation of Christians had died and there was perhaps a desire to preserve their stories. Political and social factors, however, were just as important. The Jerusalem Temple had been destroyed by the Romans in 70 CE, sending shockwaves through Jewish and Christian communities alike. And the frequent mention of persecution in Mark's Gospel may support the tradition that it was written in Rome in the aftermath of the vicious persecution of Christians by Nero only a few years before. In this turbulent atmosphere, there may well have been a need for a story of origins that brought contemporary believers face to face with the figure central to their faith.

In keeping with other ancient biographers, Mark presents Jesus' way of life to his readers and offers it as a model to follow. The focus is still very much on Jesus' Passion (meaning his suffering), almost a third of the book being devoted to his final ministry in Jerusalem and his death on the cross. Yet the earlier life of Jesus plays a much greater role here than it did in Paul. Of particular importance to Mark is the question of Jesus' identity: it is clear that he is the Messiah, and yet this has to be hidden from characters in the narrative, such that a blanket of secrecy envelops the Markan Jesus. It is only in the Passion narrative that the secrecy can be lifted and the reader understands what most characters in the story do not: that Jesus is a messiah who suffers and dies.

Mark takes up the story at Jesus' baptism, where God's heavenly voice formally acknowledges him to be his adopted Son. The Evangelist arranges his material so that the first half of the work describes Jesus' Galilean ministry, including miracles, parables and conflict with religious authorities. Jesus has power and authority even over nature: he stills storms, walks on water and possesses supernatural knowledge. The middle section starts with Jesus' glorious appearance at the Transfiguration, a scene in which Jesus displays his heavenly glory, accompanied by Elijah and Moses. It then describes a journey to Jerusalem during which Jesus both predicts his own death and outlines the cost of discipleship for those who would follow him. Disciples, he says, will have to take up their own cross, perhaps literally, and renounce all worldly honour and status. The final part of the story describes Jesus' entry into Jerusalem and his last week, outlining in some detail the final evening, his arrest, trials and crucifixion. The Gospel ends enigmatically with a group of women at the empty tomb, who run away terrified, though later audiences were unhappy with this ending and added a number of resurrection appearances (Mark 16.9–20).

This early biography of Jesus proved extremely popular, travelling widely and influencing much later literature. The Gospels of Matthew and Luke are thought to have used Mark as a major source a decade or so later, though both produce their own, distinctive portraits of Jesus.

Matthew was probably written for Christians who still considered themselves part of the Jewish synagogue or had only recently left. The Evangelist recasts Mark's Jesus within a much more recognizably Jewish context. He is presented as the Son of David, a lawgiver like Moses (Matthew 5) and throughout is continually shown to be the fulfilment of scriptural promises: this Gospel includes over 60 scriptural quotations. Matthew arranges his material so that he incorporates five blocks of teaching, reminiscent of the five books of Moses in the Torah, the most famous being the Sermon on the Mount (Matthew 5—7).

Luke continues the Gospel story into a second volume known as the Acts of the Apostles. While the Gospel charts the spread of the new faith to Jerusalem, the centre of the Jewish world, the sequel chronicles its movement to Rome, the centre of the imperial world. Clearly this Evangelist has a particular interest in bringing the Gentile mission into his story of origins. Luke's Jesus is a Spirit-filled teacher and prophet who dies simply because it is always the fate of prophets to be rejected by Israel (Luke 13.33—34). His Jesus brings salvation from political oppression (1.71, 74) and is an advocate of economic reversal and social inclusion. Luke's Gospel to the poor and outcast has resonated with many Christians through the centuries and is still relevant today.

Both Matthew and Luke provide Jesus with a genealogy. While both trace his descent through King David, Matthew tracks it ultimately to Abraham, the father of the Jewish race, while Luke tracks it to Adam, the first human. Of greater significance in the long run, however, were the miraculous accounts of his birth. It was a common assumption in the Graeco-Roman world that great men should have unconventional births. Olympias, the mother of Alexander the Great, for example, is said to have dreamt that her womb was struck by a thunderbolt, causing a flame to spread throughout her body – an indication that

Zeus was her child's father. Similarly Atia, the mother of the Emperor Augustus, is said to have been impregnated by the god Apollo in the form of a snake as she slept at his temple. Several characters in the Jewish Scriptures have notable births, being born either to an older woman, such as Sarah, in her eighties when she bore Isaac, or to someone known to be barren, such as Hannah, Samuel's mother. The unusual birth is taken to be a clear sign that the child has been specially chosen by God. Matthew and Luke draw on these conventions, but both go further than anything in the Jewish Scriptures. The mother of the Messiah wasn't simply old or barren, they maintain, but a virgin who had not yet slept with a man.

Whether the Evangelists intended their accounts of Jesus' birth to be taken as historical is anyone's guess. Both were written in the late first century, long after anyone had any reliable information about actual events. The two accounts are quite different and reconciling them is no easy task – as anyone who has ever tried to put on a nativity play will know. What the poetic language shows, however, is that the true father of Jesus was not Joseph the carpenter, but God. Moreover, Jesus did not simply become the Son of God at his baptism, as Mark's Gospel suggests, but was always God's son – from the moment of his conception. Finally, the birth at Bethlehem, the city of David, establishes his messianic credentials as one truly from the house and lineage of David.

At the other end of the story, Luke adds another event that was to prove important in the Christian view of Jesus: his ascension into heaven. This is narrated twice, once at the end of the Gospel (Luke 24.50–51) and again at the start of his second volume (Acts 1.1–11). On a purely practical level, Luke's story draws a line under the resurrection appearances and explains what happened to Jesus' resurrected body, which for Luke is a solid, physical body. More importantly, though, Luke makes it clear that Jesus has ascended to the right hand of the Father, where he is now seated in glory. Characters in Acts occasionally catch a glimpse of the exalted Jesus: Stephen sees a vision of him before he dies as the first Christian martyr (Acts 7.55–56); Paul sees and hears him on the Damascus road (Acts 9).

Turning to John's Gospel, we encounter a range of new Christian images for Jesus. Right from the prologue we learn that Jesus is the Word of God, an embodiment of divine Wisdom and the agent of God's creation. While other Gospels leave the divinity of Jesus ambiguous, John is quite clear: the Word was God (John 1.1). This Gospel stresses Jesus' pre-existence, the idea that he had a heavenly life before his earthly ministry (for an earlier articulation of this belief, see Philippians 2). And throughout his work, the Evangelist presents Jesus as the fulfilment and replacement of Jewish feasts and institutions: Jesus is the new Temple (chapter 2), the new manna in the wilderness (chapter 6) and the new paschal lamb (chapter 19). Other distinctive portraits of Jesus can be found in Hebrews, a homily exploring the cosmic significance of Jesus as heavenly High Priest, and the book of Revelation which, in a series of apocalyptic visions, adds to the rich store of Christian symbolism by casting Christ as 'first and last', the Lamb of God, divine Warrior and the one who sits on God's throne and receives worship.

Other portraits of Jesus

By the early second century, most of the documents in what would become the New Testament had been written.

There was, however, no 'New Testament' at this period, nor was there any concept of a 'canon', or body of authoritative writing. Different Christian groups presumably had their own favourites. Paul's letters and the Gospels seem to have been popular with everyone, especially Matthew's Gospel, which was pre-eminent in the early Church, but other writings were still taking shape, and as the next few centuries wore on, an ever-increasing body of Christian literature was produced.

Much of this literature was the product of pure curiosity: what was Jesus like as a child, for example? Only one of the four canonical Gospels give us a story from Jesus' childhood: discovering after a day's travel that their twelve-year-old son wasn't with them, Jesus' distraught parents return to Jerusalem only to find him discussing legal matters with teachers in the Temple. 'Did you not know that I must be in my father's house?' asks the surprised child (Luke 2.41–51). Christians naturally wanted to know more about Jesus' childhood and upbringing, and a number of writings filled in the details with legendary accounts.

One work that achieved great popularity was the *Protoevangelium of James*. This second-century prequel to the Gospels tells us about Jesus' mother Mary, including her own extraordinary conception and childhood and her great piety and perpetual virginity. The birth of Jesus is recounted at the very end of the story, where it takes place in a cave outside Bethlehem – and causes his mother no pain whatsoever! Covering somewhat later ground, the *Infancy Gospel of Thomas* recounts a number of incidents from Jesus' childhood. In one, he gives life to clay birds on the Sabbath but in others he is a menace, wielding God-like powers with the petulance of a child. At the other end of the story, we find letters from Pilate to the emperor explaining his actions, transcripts of Jesus' trial and accounts of the deaths of the disciples. Of particular interest are the *Gospel of Peter*, which describes the resurrection itself and memorably features a walking, talking cross, and the *Gospel of Nicodemus*, which recounts Jesus' descent into Hades on Easter Saturday and his preaching to the dead.

Much of this literature was perfectly orthodox, providing simple, pious fiction for the faithful until well into the Middle Ages. While lacking any great theological sophistication, these texts nevertheless proved highly influential in shaping popular conceptions of Jesus and other actors in the Christian drama. The *Protoevangelium of James*, for example, played an important role in emerging Marian devotion, and the *Gospel of Nicodemus* provided a written account of an event popularized by the medieval mystery plays and known as the 'harrowing of hell'.

Another body of literature, however, was more threatening, at least to the church fathers of the second century and beyond. These were the writings of the Gnostics. Influenced by Greek philosophy, Gnostics held a dualistic view of the universe, with the realm of light, goodness and spirit on one side, and darkness, evil and matter on the other. The Supreme God belonged to the heavenly realm of light, but humans were trapped in the world of darkness, created by a lesser god known as the Demiurge. In order to ascend to the realm of light, people needed knowledge (or *gnōsis* in Greek, hence 'gnostic'). Not all Gnostics were Christian, but those who were produced a number of esoteric texts, some of which were found in a jar in the Egyptian town of Nag Hammadi in 1945. Of note here are the *Gospel of Philip*, the *Gospel of Truth* and the *Dialogue of the Saviour*.

Gnostic-Christian texts tend to cover two major topics. The first is speculation on Jesus' existence *before* he entered the world, and the texts often include complicated cosmologies designed to explain how the Supreme God could take on corrupt human flesh. Generally speaking, however, the gulf between the world of light and earthly matter was too wide, and most Gnostics believed that Jesus only *seemed* to be a real human and so did not really suffer and die – a point that was to put them at odds with the emerging orthodox view. The second area of interest focuses on the secret teaching of the risen Jesus, providing readers with the necessary knowledge to enable the soul to ascend to its true heavenly home.

Probably the best-known gnostic text is the *Gospel of Thomas* – not to be confused with the infancy gospel of the same name mentioned above. This second-century document contains 114 verses, most of which are sayings of Jesus given in secret to Thomas. Some of these are very similar to the kind of things we read in the New Testament Gospels. For example:

> Jesus said, 'Look, the sower went out, took a handful (of seeds), and scattered (them). Some fell on the road, and the birds came and gathered them. Others fell on rock, and they didn't take root in the soil and didn't produce heads of grain. Others fell on thorns, and they choked the seeds and worms ate them. And others fell on good soil, and it produced a good crop: it yielded sixty per measure and one hundred and twenty per measure.'   (*Gospel of Thomas*, 9)

Other sections are very different:

> Jesus said to them, 'When you make the two into one, and when you make the inner like the outer and the outer like

the inner, and the upper like the lower, and when you make
male and female into a single one, so that the male will not
be male nor the female be female, when you make eyes in
place of an eye, a hand in place of a hand, a foot in place of
a foot, an image in place of an image, then you will enter
[the kingdom].'   (*Gospel of Thomas*, 22)

Like other gnostic works, there is nothing in this gospel on
Jesus' suffering, death or even resurrection. Salvation is not
through Jesus' death on the cross but through the acquisition of secret knowledge.

The church fathers were strident in their critique of these
gospels, but Gnosticism wasn't for everyone, and the most
popular Gospels in the early Church remained the four we
now find in the New Testament. Ironically, perhaps, it was
in the fight against groups later branded as 'heretics' that
the New Testament began to take shape. From the mass of
Christian literature now available, church leaders sought
to put together a group of authoritative, trustworthy texts
that the faithful could read without peril. Rather than
imposing works from the top down, however, they tended
to favour texts that had already achieved a measure of
popularity. The formation of a canon was a slow process,
and it was not until the fourth century that a collection
that we would recognize emerged. In his festal letter of
367, Bishop Athanasius of Alexandria listed 27 texts in
which 'the teaching of godliness is proclaimed' – exactly
the same texts that are found in the New Testament.
Athanasius' list was not the final word, however. Some still
wanted to exclude the book of Revelation and a number
of letters, while others wanted to include the *Shepherd of
Hermas* and the *Epistle of Barnabas*. Still, it was a significant step in the movement towards establishing a canon,

and it meant that the portrait of Jesus found in these 27 works – and only these 27 – would increasingly be regarded as authoritative.

Jesus the God

The first three centuries were a difficult time for the early Church, which found itself at the centre of sporadic persecution by decree of either the emperor or local governors. A decisive step in its fortunes, however, came with the accession of Constantine, the first Christian emperor, who reigned from 306 to 337. He was responsible for the Edict of Milan in 313, guaranteeing toleration for Christians throughout the Empire. He also ordered the building of the church of the Holy Sepulchre on the site of Jesus' tomb, a place that was to become one of the holiest sites in Christendom.

It was in the reign of Constantine that the Church began a series of councils, aimed at articulating Christian belief. The figure of Jesus posed particular problems: how could Jesus be both a human creature, obedient to the Father and subject to normal human limitations, and yet at the same time God? In 325, a large number of bishops from throughout the Roman Empire gathered in Nicaea to give their attention to what was known as the 'Arian controversy'. An Alexandrian presbyter named Arius so emphasized the supremacy and uniqueness of God the Father that he tended to downgrade the Son. The Son, he claimed, was created by the Father, the first and most perfect of God's creatures. The implication of this was that the Son had a beginning, unlike the Father, and so was not eternal. He was sharply opposed by the Bishop of Alexandria, who argued that the Son was 'eternally begotten' by the Father from his own being, that the two were one in both being and purpose, and that the two were co-eternal. Both sides could appeal to Christian writings in support of their views, often from the same texts. Arius, for example, could cite John 14.28 ('for the Father is greater than I'), while his opponents could point to John 10.30 ('I and the Father are one'). In the end, the decision went overwhelmingly against Arius. The council declared the Son to be the true God, co-eternal with him and begotten from his same substance. Their formulation was expressed in the Nicene Creed, a statement of faith still used by Christians today.

> We believe in one Lord, Jesus Christ,
> the only Son of God,
> eternally begotten of the Father,
> God from God, Light from Light,
> true God from true God,
> begotten, not made,
> of one Being with the Father.
> Through him all things were made.
>
> For us and for our salvation
> he came down from heaven:
> by the power of the Holy Spirit
> he became incarnate from the Virgin Mary,
> and was made man.
>
> For our sake he was crucified under Pontius Pilate;
> he suffered death and was buried.
> On the third day he rose again
> in accordance with the Scriptures;
> he ascended into heaven
> and is seated at the right hand of the Father.

He will come again in glory to judge the living and
  the dead,
and his kingdom will have no end.[5]

Subsequent councils fine-tuned this description, the
Council of Chalcedon (431 CE) famously describing Christ
as 'fully God and fully human'. This quickly became the
mainstream Christian view of Jesus, and has remained so
within most denominations ever since.

These debates and controversies underline just how far
the Church had travelled from its Hebraic roots within just
a few centuries. By the fifth century, the figure of Jesus was
firmly understood within Greek philosophical concepts
relating to his divine being, nature and substance. The
Jewish prophet from Nazareth was now worshipped by his
followers as God incarnate.

7

Art, relics, passion plays – and even time itself

We ended the last chapter in the rarefied world of Christian intellectuals and their councils in the fourth and fifth centuries. But as the centuries passed, how did ordinary people relate to Jesus, particularly as Christianity became dominant in Europe throughout the Middle Ages? In this chapter we shall consider a range of ways people related to the figure of Jesus – through pilgrimage, the cult of relics, mystery plays and even the divisions of time. First, though, we'll ask what image people had of the founder of their faith.

Jesus in art

Curiously perhaps, the Gospels give us no description of what Jesus looked like. We might have expected to be told that he was handsome with beautiful eyes, like King David before him (1 Samuel 16), but the Evangelists remain remarkably silent on the issue. The book of Revelation gives a terrifying account of the risen Jesus, featuring white hair, fiery eyes and brazen feet (Revelation 1), but this is no help whatsoever in picturing the man from Nazareth. Most of the early church fathers simply assumed that Jesus had been physically beautiful, though others promoted an 'ugly Jesus'. Some who held this view were opponents of Christianity, such as Celsus, who described Jesus as 'ugly and small'. Others, such as Tertullian and Irenaeus, drew inspiration from the prophet Isaiah, who foretold the uncomely appearance of God's Servant (Isaiah 53).

Perhaps because of the Jewish ban on graven images (Exodus 20), artistic representations of Jesus took a while to appear. The earliest Christians preferred to draw on a range of symbols to denote Christ and their allegiance to him. Best known is the fish symbol, where the Greek word for fish, *ichthus*, spells the first letters of various key Christian terms:

I   *Iēsous* (Jesus)
Ch   *Christos* (Christ)
Th   *Theos* (God)
U   *huios* (Son)
S   *Soter* (Saviour)

Later on, the Chi-Rho symbol also became popular, standing for the two Greek letters that start the name 'Christ': Chi (χ) and rho (ρ), giving ☧.

The earliest Christian portraits of Jesus come from the church at Dura-Europos in Syria and date to shortly before 250 CE. The church contains three paintings of Christ, as the good shepherd, healing the paralytic and walking on water with Peter. In each of these, Jesus is presented as a young philosopher, with short hair, tunic and cloak. Similar paintings emerged in the catacombs in Rome, now paying particular attention to Jesus' baptism, the raising of Lazarus and the Last Supper. And from the fifth century onwards, two-dimensional painted icons became popular in the Eastern Church, drawing inspiration particularly from Jesus' glorious appearance at the Transfiguration.

The familiar portrait of Christ on the cross took some time to develop, largely because of the intense revulsion associated with crucifixion and its victims. Its earliest attestation is actually in the context of an insult. It takes the form of a crudely drawn graffito, found on the Palatine Hill in Rome, and dating to around the third century. It depicts a donkey-headed man on a cross, accompanied by a man with a hand raised in praise and the words 'Alexamenos worships his God'. As pagans often linked the Jewish God with a donkey in antiquity, the whole scene is clearly meant to ridicule a Christian believer by the name of Alexamenos. It was not until the fourth century that Christians were able to reclaim the image of the cross and make it central in their iconography. Under Constantine, crucifixion was banned, and with the finding of the 'true cross' by Constantine's mother Helena, and the rise of pilgrimage to the newly established church of the Holy Sepulchre, the image of Christ on the cross steadily grew in popularity. By the thirteenth century a crucifixion scene – whether a painting or a crucifix – formed the focal point of every church altar. This is still the case in most Catholic churches, though since the Reformation, Protestant churches have favoured an empty cross, as a symbol of the resurrection.

The life of Jesus provided rich material for artists throughout the ages and forms the bedrock of the Western artistic tradition. Nativity scenes were popularized by St Francis of Assisi in the late twelfth century, and were particularly widespread in southern Europe in the centuries that followed. Leonardo da Vinci produced a physically beautiful Jesus in his famous portrait of the Last Supper in the late 1400s, and a century later Caravaggio split public opinion with his naturalistic interpretations of biblical scenes. Although a standard portrait as a bearded man with flowing hair did gradually develop, most artists presented a Jesus who conformed to their own cultural stereotypes, both in dress and appearance. It was not until the twentieth century that artists displayed an awareness of Jesus' 'otherness', not only in portraiture but also in plays and films (see below).

Pilgrimage and relics

With the rise of pilgrimage in the fourth century and beyond, sacred sites and saintly relics came to occupy an increasingly important place in Christian piety. Jerusalem was an obvious draw, but so too was Rome with its tombs of Peter and Paul, and Santiago de Compostela in Spain, the final resting place – it was claimed – of James, the son of Zebedee. By the eighth century, relics of some sort or another were to be found in most Christian churches, and it was widely believed that the saints associated with them might perform miracles, perhaps curing illness or interceding on behalf of the faithful in heaven. Some of the more successful shrines were a source of great income to the surrounding community, with throngs of visitors contributing to the local economy.

In 326–8, the Empress Helena, the mother of Constantine, made a pilgrimage to the Holy Land, where she is said to have found wood from the cross of Christ along with some of the nails used at the crucifixion. Not surprisingly, these became some of the holiest relics of Christendom, and a number of other items from the Passion appeared in the courts of Europe over the next few centuries. A pillar on which Jesus was said to have been scourged was known from at least the third century, and a crown of thorns that appeared in the fifth century, was eventually acquired by Louis IX of France and is now in Notre-Dame Cathedral in Paris. Of great importance to the Holy Roman Empire was the Holy Lance, the spear used to pierce Jesus' side at the crucifixion and said to be embellished with one of the nails from the cross; as a symbol of power and authority, kings and emperors took it into battle with them and kept it closely guarded. And the cup from the Last Supper also acquired a special status, particularly once it was linked with the Holy Grail legends in the Middle Ages. Of course, establishing the authenticity of any of these 'relics' has never been easy. In the sixteenth century Erasmus wrote sarcastically about the number of buildings that could be made from fragments of the 'true cross'. At least 30 crucifixion nails were in existence by the early 1900s, and museums and basilicas currently boast at least four Holy Lances.

Unlike the saints, Jesus had ascended into heaven, meaning that no bodily remains were available. The only exception to this was his foreskin, which was removed at his circumcision. Rather bizarrely perhaps, a number of churches claimed to possess this and to have benefited from the miraculous powers associated with it. According to the apocryphal *Arabic Infancy Gospel*, the old Hebrew woman who performed the circumcision preserved the foreskin in an alabaster box full of expensive oil – the very same oil that 'Mary the sinner' later poured over Jesus and wiped with her hair (Luke 7). On Christmas Day in 800 CE, the Emperor Charlemagne gave Christ's foreskin to Pope Leo III at his coronation. Charlemagne apparently claimed that an angel gave it to him when he prayed at the Holy Sepulchre, though another account says it was a wedding gift from a

Byzantine empress. Several other foreskins appeared across Europe, though most disappeared after the Reformation, and the one that had originally been given to Leo III was stolen in the 1980s.

Perhaps the most significant relic associated with Jesus, however, is the Shroud of Turin, believed by many to be the cloth wrapped around him at his burial. The long piece of linen contains two faint sepia images of a naked man (front and back), with his hands crossed over his genitals and with the long hair and beard associated with portraits of Jesus. Radiocarbon dating carried out in 1988 suggested that the cloth dates from the Middle Ages, which coincides quite neatly with its first appearance in France in 1357. Despite this, the 'shroud' continues to attract millions of visitors, including Pope John Paul II and Pope Benedict XVI.

Roughly contemporaneous with the cult of relics in medieval Europe were the hugely popular mystery plays. At first they were performed in the churches, but when, in the early thirteenth century, Pope Innocent III forbade clergy to participate in them, they were taken on by town guilds. From then on they were performed in the vernacular rather than Latin, non-biblical scenes were added and the whole performance became more elaborate, often lasting several days and adopting an irreverent tone. Some attempted the broad sweep of biblical history, from creation to judgement day, while others were more focused, the Passion being a particular favourite at Easter.

One of the most famous passion plays was first performed at Oberammergau in Bavaria in 1634. During a plague, the residents of the town are said to have promised God that they would put on a play every ten years if he spared them. In the end, the town didn't succumb to the epidemic and the play has been performed every decade since. It has been rewritten several times, most recently in response to charges of anti-Semitism, but even today attracts thousands of pilgrims.

Time

The ancient Church always had a particular interest in the calendar and dating systems. This was largely because its major feast, Easter, required a certain amount of complicated reckoning to transpose a *solar* reference point – Easter was celebrated on the first Sunday after the first full moon on or after the spring equinox – on to the *lunar* calendars in use throughout the Roman world.

Christians from Luke onwards had simply adopted the Roman system of dating events by the reign of emperors – a system that itself went back to the founding of Rome under Romulus and Remus. By the early sixth century, the most common dating system was based on the years of Diocletian; since this emperor had been a persecutor of the early Church, however, this was not an ideal situation. In 525, Dionysius Exiguus ('Dennis the Small', or perhaps 'Humble'), a Scythian monk living in Rome, worked out an entirely new dating system, counting from the annunciation of Christ's birth. Years would now be designated Anno Domini (AD), or 'year of our Lord'.

It is not quite clear how Dionysius went about his calculations, and many modern scholars think he got the date of the annunciation wrong. The Gospels, however, do not give us an exact date for the events surrounding Jesus' nativity. Luke links it with the census under Quirinius that took place in 6 CE. More commonly, scholars rely on Matthew's dating, which suggests that Jesus was born shortly before the death of Herod (4 BCE), perhaps around 6 BCE. A date somewhere in the middle of these two possibilities may not be all that far off the mark, and is perhaps as much as we can achieve at this distance from events.

The new calendar took a little time to catch on. It was used by the English historian the Venerable Bede in his *Ecclesiastical History of the English People*, completed in 731, and Alcuin of York introduced the system to the Carolingian Empire some decades later, thereby spreading it throughout western Europe. It was not until the fourteenth century that it was firmly adopted by Catholic Europe, however, Portugal being the last to change in 1422. And it was only from 1700, the year Russia relinquished the old Byzantine calendar, that it was adopted by the Eastern Orthodox Church. The effect of this change was to situate the life of Christ as a turning point in history, world events now being measured according to whether they occurred before or after his birth. Although Jews and Muslims have their own systems, the calendar remains the most widely used dating system today. In recent times, however, some have become uncomfortable with its explicitly Christian orientation and have replaced AD and BC with CE and BCE ('Common Era' and 'Before the Common Era'), a convention adopted in this book. The dates are identical; only the designation has changed.

Jesus' life has also left its mark on divisions within the year. Years are divided up in many countries by Christian feasts, predominantly Christmas and Easter. Schools, universities and often governmental terms are arranged around Christian holidays, and a host of other, smaller Christian festivals punctuate the calendar: Ascension, Whitsun, saints' days and so on. While the latter may be increasingly disappearing from the more secular countries of northern Europe, they remain part of the social landscape in the predominantly Catholic countries of the south.

In the next chapter we shall turn our attention to the influence of Jesus today, both among believers and among those who profess no particular Christian adherence.

8

Jesus today

Jesus' greatest legacy is, of course, the Christian Church. With over 2.2 billion adherents throughout the world, amounting to a third of the people on earth, the movement that Jesus inspired is truly global. In this final chapter we shall consider not only the Christian religion but also Jesus' place in other world religions, along with his strangely enduring role in the increasingly secular West.

Contemporary Christianity

The Church has always been associated with missionary activity – from the spread of the new faith to Rome in the book of Acts, through to the evangelization of the 'new world' in the great 'age of discovery' in the fifteenth to the eighteenth centuries. Hot on the heels of European exploration and colonial conquest went Christian missionaries, often forcibly converting indigenous peoples, resulting in a variety of beliefs as older traditional ideas incorporated the new faith.

Today the areas of greatest growth are largely to be found in Africa, the former Soviet bloc and China. Christianity is more firmly rooted in the Global South than in the West, which, faced with increasing secularization, has seen a distinct turning away from 'organized religion' – a point we shall come back to below. In many respects this represents a return to an earlier phase of the Church. Christianity was never a 'European' religion: the earliest church fathers were largely North African; Christian monasticism started in Egypt; and before the emergence of Islam, Christians had a large presence in Iran, Afghanistan, Yemen, Saudi Arabia and most central Asian countries. The apostle Thomas is said to have taken the faith to India, and the Church made inroads into China and Mongolia relatively early. Ironically perhaps, missionaries now come from Africa, Latin America and East Asia to the West.

Churches that have seen particular growth over recent decades tend to be the Evangelical and Pentecostal ones, with their stress on the authority of the Bible and the need for believers to be 'born again'. Both groups are particularly strong in the USA and the Global South, and are often associated with theologically conservative positions on questions of gender and sexuality.

Through all its differing manifestations, the Church has continued to promote the life, death and example of Jesus Christ. Readings from the Gospels recall stories from his life, prayers ask him to intervene with his heavenly Father, and sermons ponder the meaning of his words for life today. A popular Evangelical youth movement in the USA in the 1990s promoted wristbands on which were written 'WWJD' – 'What Would Jesus Do?' The point of the wristbands was to encourage young people to base their morality on the life and love of Christ, something that goes back, of course, to the ancient idea of 'imitation of Christ' enshrined in the Gospels themselves.

Alongside all this, a lively tradition of hymn singing also characterizes most Christian churches. The Reformation produced two different reactions to hymns. One response was to reject anything that wasn't biblical, including hymn singing and music in churches – only psalms and plainchant were allowed. An alternative approach, championed particularly by Martin Luther, produced a burst of hymn writing and congregational singing. Gradually hymns emerged that didn't simply paraphrase Scripture: the Methodist Charles Wesley was famous for writing over 6,000 hymns, including 'Hark the Herald Angels Sing'; the 'Second Great Awakening' in the USA in the early nineteenth century led to an explosion of sacred music, including 'Amazing Grace' and 'How Great Thou Art'; African Americans produced distinctive spirituals; and contemporary worship over the last few decades has been very much influenced by popular music. Hymns, like poems, allow their authors great scope for contemplating both the character of Jesus and the Christian response to him today.

Jesus in Islam

Christianity is not, however, the only world religion to revere Jesus: he also plays a prominent role within Islam. This is perhaps not particularly surprising, given that Islam emerged in close proximity to both Jews and Christians, and attracted converts and controversies from both faiths. Portraits of Jesus found within Islam show influence from the full range of Jesus literature available by the early seventh century – not only the canonical Gospels but apocryphal and gnostic ones too.

Jesus is actually a major figure within Islam, mentioned in 15 out of the Qur'an's 114 chapters. He is considered a prophet of the highest rank, a messenger or *rasul* who brings a book (the gospel), alongside Abraham, Moses and

Muhammad. Although the Qur'an mentions Jesus' miraculous conception, he is not considered divine. He is called the 'Spirit of God' because he was born through the action of the Spirit and performs miracles through the power of God. Jesus was not actually crucified, though it looked that way to unbelievers; instead, he was physically raised to the heavens at the ascension, which for most Muslims is the major event in his life. Most believe that he will return to earth at the end of time and defeat the anti-Christ, *ad-Dajjal*. Very little of Jesus' teaching is preserved, perhaps because Muslims consider that the Gospels have lost Jesus' authentic message, such that Muhammad needed to come later to restore it. In this way, Jesus is very much seen as a precursor to Muhammad himself.

Jesus in Judaism

Within Judaism, perceptions of Jesus tend to be much more hostile. Once again there are good historical reasons for this: we saw in Part 1 that several sections of the New Testament are anti-Jewish, and the two faiths split from one another amid often acrimonious controversy. Throughout the Middle Ages, passion plays presented Jews as Christ-killers, stoking the fires of Christian anti-Semitism, leading to hostility and suspicion and eventually anti-Jewish pogroms. Jewish rabbis saw Jesus as an apostate, a sorcerer who proclaimed himself to be divine. An extremely popular medieval Jewish tract known as the *Toledot Yeshu* (*The History of Jesus*) claimed that Mary was raped by Joseph Pandera (possibly a Roman soldier); that Jesus performed miracles by the power of God's name, which he had smuggled out of the Temple; that the Jewish leaders charged him with sorcery and leading followers astray; and that his body was later taken by a gardener and buried elsewhere (hence the empty tomb).

From the nineteenth century onwards, however, Jewish scholars began to take an interest in the historical Jesus, reclaiming him as 'Jesus the Jew' and regarding him as someone who merited a place in Jewish literature alongside other ancient sages. It became clear that Jesus did not want to found a new religion, that he was law-observant to the last and that he actually had much more in common with the Pharisees than the Gospels tend to suggest. In the wake of the Holocaust, much work has been done on Jesus' crucifixion. It is now generally acknowledged that primary responsibility for Jesus' death rested with the Romans and that the charge was not blasphemy but sedition. The Christian tendency to blame 'the Jews' for Jesus' death is now seen as inaccurate; at most a small group of Jewish leaders handed Jesus over to the Romans, and even here there were doubtless good reasons for what they did. In 1965 the Second Vatican Council formally dismissed the idea that Jews were to blame for Jesus' death and were thus rejected by God. This has led to better relations between the two groups, which are now more likely to be seen as 'sibling faiths' rather than rivals.

Cultural Christians

As already noted, the rise of secularism has led to a turning away from organized religion in certain areas, particularly the north and west of Europe. While some are happy to embrace atheism or to declare themselves agnostics, there has been a rise in the number of people describing themselves as 'cultural Christians', those who neither accept the theological beliefs of the Church nor look to Christ as a saviour figure but, as a result of growing up within a broadly Christian society, are happy to identify themselves with Christian *culture* in the same way that non-practising Muslims and Jews might appeal to their distinctive cultural traditions. Christian feasts, hymns, nativity plays and requiem masses are all part of our shared cultural context, and one does not have to be a practising Christian to find them socially relevant or even spiritually moving.

While the Church often fares badly in much modern secular discourse, the figure of Jesus of Nazareth has proved remarkably resilient. He continues to be held up as a great moral teacher and example to others, even by people with no particular Christian belief. Like Mahatma Gandhi, he is commonly regarded as a genuinely good man with a strong moral outlook.

In an age of declining biblical literacy, most people nowadays derive their knowledge of Jesus from films and other media. Within the English-speaking world, Franco Zeffirelli's six-hour television miniseries *Jesus of Nazareth* was a significant milestone in 1977. Reaching audiences in the hundreds of millions worldwide, the actor Robert Powell's blue-eyed ethereal figure defined the image of Jesus for a generation. Two years later, and using the same set as Zeffirelli, *Monty Python's Life of Brian* (1979) set an altogether more irreverent tone. Although the producers were careful to distinguish between the Christ figure – who appears only a couple of times – and the hapless Brian, the similarities between their stories ensured that the film would be surrounded by controversy from the beginning. More recently, Mel Gibson's *The Passion of the Christ* (2004) caused an outcry both because of its violence and its frequent anti-Jewishness. Of course, crucifixion *was* brutal, probably even more so than Gibson portrayed; and the anti-Jewish tone stems from the Gospels themselves, particularly in the Passion narratives. Nevertheless both aspects of the film offended modern sensibilities.

The question of Jesus' relationship to Mary Magdalene continues to be of great popular interest. In 1970 it was explored in a sensitive manner by Andrew Lloyd Webber and Tim Rice in their rock opera *Jesus Christ Superstar*, where a doting Mary sings of her love for Jesus. Much more controversially, Martin Scorsese's *The Last Temptation* (1988), based on Nikos Kazantzakis' novel *The Last Temptation of Christ*, depicted a dying Jesus tempted by Satan to come down from the cross, marry Mary Magdalene and live a normal family life. Although Jesus resists temptation, the film caused a scandal and was banned in many countries for several years. Similar themes were taken up and developed in Ron Howard's *The Da Vinci Code* (2006), based on Dan Brown's bestselling novel of the same title, where Jesus and Mary have a child, establishing a bloodline that runs through the Merovingian kings of France and on to the present day. The central characters are caught up in an implausible web of intrigue involving Vatican conspiracies and a host of 'usual suspects' – the Priory of Sion, Opus Dei, the Knights Templar and legends of the Holy Grail. At present, 'swords and sandals' films show no signs of abating – the History Channel's ten-hour adaptation of *The Bible* and its film spin-off, *Son of God* (2014), are only the latest manifestations.

Perhaps more intriguing than adaptations of the life of Jesus, however, are novels and films that tap into a powerful

'Christ myth'. In these a good and virtuous character often sacrifices him- or herself for others and ends up dying in a manner reminiscent of crucifixion, perhaps with arms outstretched or with words of forgiveness. A well-known example of this is Aslan in C. S. Lewis' series of novels The Chronicles of Narnia, where the Christian imagery is overt. Less conspicuous, though still frequently following this narrative arc, are J. K. Rowling's Harry Potter novels, J. R. R. Tolkien's Gandalf, Neo in the *Matrix* film trilogy, John Connor in the *Terminator* film series and often the Doctor in the very long-running UK television series *Doctor Who*. While most of these could not be described as 'Christian' (a recent *Doctor Who* writer, for example, is an atheist), their plotline follows a distinctively Christian scheme – one so fundamental to most people brought up in Christian countries that we hardly notice it.

Postscript: Christ the Redeemer

In the summer of 2016, the Olympic Games were held in the Brazilian city of Rio de Janeiro. Standing high above on the Corcovado Mountain and overlooking the city is the huge Art Deco statue of Christ the Redeemer. With his arms outstretched, the statue symbolizes not just Christ's care and protection of the people down below but Christianity throughout the world. As thousands of people watched the games, and millions more tuned in on their television sets, the figure of Christ was a constant, if sometimes peripheral, presence.

In many respects the statue sums up the subject of this book. Born in a rural backwater, Jesus' message of the imminent arrival of God's kingdom got him into trouble with the political authorities of his day. He was betrayed by a friend, arrested and executed, with little in the way of a formal trial. But that was not the end of his story. Three days later his followers claimed that he had been raised from the dead and exalted to glory, and that conviction, and its implications, only became stronger with the passage of time. Two thousand years later, many are still drawn to this enigmatic figure. For some he is an abiding presence who calls them to worship; others hold him in respect as a great teacher and moral example; and even those with no particular interest find themselves bombarded by his image and legacy. One thing is certain: without Jesus of Nazareth, modern society would look very different.

Glossary

apocalyptic takes its name from a type of literature containing visions and revelations to do with the end times. An 'apocalyptic prophet' is one who announces impending judgement

chief priests aristocratic Jerusalem priests responsible for the day-to-day running of Judaea. The High Priest was chosen from their number

Gentiles non-Jews

Gnosticism a philosophical system popular from the second century CE; for Christian Gnostics, salvation came through the acquisition of secret knowledge

Gospel the term originally meant 'good news' but came to denote a specifically Christian work presenting the life, ministry and death of Jesus, or part of it

Hasmonaeans Jewish High Priest-Kings of the second/first century BCE; descended from the Maccabees

Herod I (also known as Herod the Great) Idumaean Jew put on throne by Rome, ruled from 37 BCE to 4 BCE

Josephus aristocratic Jewish general and historian, 37–c.100 CE. Almost everything we know about Judaea in this period comes from Josephus' two works, *The Jewish War* and the *Antiquities of the Jews*

Passion this comes from the Latin word for 'suffering' and is commonly used for the suffering of Christ as depicted in the Gospels. The concluding chapters of the Gospels are often referred to as the 'Passion narratives'

Pharisees a Jewish sect known for their interest in purity, biblical interpretation and oral traditions

prefect   title of the Roman governor of Judaea

purity   the state in which a person is ready to enter the holy Temple of God. Many things can make a person impure (or unclean): contact with an impure person or thing, e.g. a corpse, bodily emissions. Ritual washing usually restores purity

Son of Man   a phrase Jesus often used to refer to himself. On one level it simply means 'I', but it may also have deliberately evoked the end-time figure of Daniel 7

Temple   located in Jerusalem and sole cultic centre for the worship of the Jewish God. The Second Temple was built after the return from exile and refurbished on a lavish scale by Herod I

Torah   the Jewish law. Sometimes refers specifically to the first five books of the Bible: Genesis, Exodus, Leviticus, Numbers and Deuteronomy

Transfiguration   a scene described in Mark 9.2–8 (also Matthew 17.1–8 and Luke 9.28–36) in which Jesus goes up a mountain with his closest followers and appears to them in his heavenly glory, with white garments and accompanied by Moses and Elijah

Notes

1 Tacitus, *Annals*, 15.44. Loeb Classical Library vol. 322, trans. John Jackson (Cambridge, MA: Harvard University Press, 1989), p. 283.
2 Josephus, *Jewish Antiquities*, 18.63–64. Loeb Classical Library vol. 433, trans. Louis H. Feldmann (Cambridge, MA: Harvard University Press, 1965), pp. 49–51; emphasis added.
3 Philo, *On the Embassy to Gaius*, sections 144–5. Loeb Classical Library vol. 379, trans. F. H. Colson (Cambridge, MA: Harvard University Press, 1962), p. 73.
4 A papyrus fragment containing a few words of Coptic in which Jesus referred to Mary as 'my wife' came to light in 2012. Known popularly as the 'Gospel of Jesus' Wife', the fragment is currently thought to be a forgery.
5 Extract from <http://anglicansonline.org/basics/nicene.html>.

Further reading

Beilby, J. K. and Eddy, P. R., *The Historical Jesus: Five Views* (London: SPCK, 2009).

Bond, H. K., *Jesus: A Guide for the Perplexed* (London: Bloomsbury, 2012).

Brooke, G. J., *The Birth of Jesus: Biblical and Theological Reflections* (Edinburgh: T. & T. Clark, 2000).

Corley, K. E., *Women and the Historical Jesus: Feminist Myths of Christian Origins* (Santa Rosa, CA: Polebridge, 2002).

Crossan, J. D., *Jesus: A Revolutionary Biography* (San Francisco: HarperSanFrancisco, 1994).

Ehrman, B. D., *The New Testament: A Historical Introduction to the Early Christian Writings*, 5th edn (Oxford: Oxford University Press, 2011).

Eve, E., *The Healer from Nazareth: Jesus' Miracles in Historical Context* (London: SPCK, 2009).

Farhadian, C. (ed.), *Introducing World Christianity* (Oxford: Wiley-Blackwell, 2012).

Fisk, B. N., *A Hitchhiker's Guide to Jesus: Reading the Gospels on the Ground* (Grand Rapids, MI: Baker, 2011).

Fredriksen, P., *Jesus of Nazareth: King of the Jews* (New York: Vintage, 1999).

Johnson, L. T., *The Real Jesus: The Misguided Quest for the Historical Jesus and the Truth of the Traditional Gospels* (San Francisco: HarperSanFrancisco, 1996).

Lincoln, A. T., *Born of a Virgin? Reconceiving Jesus in the Bible, Tradition and Theology* (London: SPCK, 2013).

Pelikan, J., *Jesus Through the Centuries: His Place in the History of Culture*, new edn (New Haven, CT: Yale University Press, 1999).

Sanders, E. P., *The Historical Figure of Jesus* (London: Penguin, 1996).

Tatum, W. B., *Jesus: A Brief History* (Oxford: Wiley-Blackwell, 2009).

Taylor, J. E. (ed.), *Jesus and Brian: Exploring the Historical Jesus and his Times via Monty Python's Life of Brian* (London: Bloomsbury, 2015).

Van Voorst, R. E., *Jesus Outside the New Testament: An Introduction to the Ancient Evidence* (Grand Rapids, MI: Eerdmans, 2000).

Index

Index

Index